Seasons

Nicholas Olah

ISBN: 9798419485952

Table of Contents

New Year

It's a new year and I am hopeful.

The air is pure
and the ground has been painted
a fresh coat of white.

The child across the street is laughing
as she makes snow angels;
from here, it sounds
like prayer.

Morning Light

I'm in love with the way
morning light spills
hope

the way it bends
to me

the way it fills spaces
where words
won't suffice.

Reckless

There is something reckless
in your eyes tonight
and,
simply put,
I can't wait any longer
to wade in.

World on a String

To think:

we could have held all of this
with such reverence, letting the breeze
move through—

the world on a string
in our hands.

Shape of Grief

I wade knee-deep into the water,
tongue-tied in a silence that is hollow
but still heavy somehow.

Waves crash-land in the shape of grief;
they lunge at me, reach for me.

They reach and they reach.

This is Me Saying Please

I beg of you:

pull me away
from these hardened edges
and

    don't.

        let.

            go.

Spring Haiku

The morning sky breaks
May's first sun opens her eyes
I greet it, smiling

Enough

I dreamt about you
last night.

I dreamt that we weren't
everything but we were
something.

I dreamt that it was
enough.

You

There was wet concrete
and cold light
from tired stars
trying to lead me home.

There were maps
with pins in places
where I've been;
pins in places where I've left
pieces of myself.

And there was you,
and there was you.

Quiet

The morning is quiet—
a perfect metaphor
for peace.

Soft

There are storms stalking the horizon
in skies that are all gray and bruised,
all reckless and broken.

With tired eyes,
I scour the landscape for
a soft place to land

a soft place to put down
the weight
of my worries

a soft place
to rest my head
and sleep the day away.

Sunday Mornings

On Sunday mornings,
we inhale unknowns
and exhale unease.

We let our hearts bruise
like apples

carry all the hope we can fit
in our hands

wait for the dust to settle
like snow over
a city.

(The waiting is *always* the hardest part.)

River's Bend

I have left so many lies
at the river's bend
that the ripples
almost know me
by name.

Baptism

I close my eyes,
drink you in   drink your breath
like it's holy water—

and I feel saved.

Love as a Hurricane

Again and again,
love tosses and turns us
like an angry sea.

Again and again,
I wake to echoes
of our warring hearts.

And every time,
the blood leaves
my body

like it's the first time.

Summer Observations

Storms are coming.
Birds are scattering.

All of this or none of it
could be a metaphor—

even I can't know for sure.

Lightning Strike

You are the lightning
and I am the ground:

I survive
every time you strike
but am always a little less than
I was before.

The Trying

I may never learn to paint
with the colors of my bruises,

but it's all in the trying.

And I'll *die* trying—
if I have to.

Midsummer's Eve

After the storm,
I gather fruit felled by
wind-shaken branches.

Dusk peels back
the bruised-peach sky,
revealing paralyzing darkness
or shimmering stars—

all depending upon
your point of view.

Destinations

My love
was a highway
and darling—

you missed the exit.

Discretion

I move through the season
with discretion—
hushed as morning's first light,
fragile as whispered last words.

I disturb neither the tides
nor the dreaming; I do not shake
the universe awake.

I walk softly and slowly,
take what is handed me
that can be called
good—

and leave the rest.

Hints of Autumn

The calendar still says August

but I can see my breath
this morning
and the air smells like
October

and I'm here for it.

Simple

It's simple:
stretch every wall
of your heart
and
let me in.

Waiting in Suburbia

I step out onto
sunbaked surfaces—
the humidity stealing my breath.

American flags hang and flutter,
dogs bark freely.

I may never find the answers here,
but I'm learning to be content
with the wonder that comes
with the waiting.

September Seventh, Dusk

I drink the last of the evening's light,
covet each drop
like it will hydrate my body
and save my soul.

Cotton candy skies
pass over;
another summer day dies a slow
but somehow breathtaking
death.

Truth Serum

Every time I see the whites
of your eyes
I freeze

and fall in love

Storm Surge

I am still learning
how to survive the storms
that are brewed
at my hand

Farewell, Summer

September swoops in, strangles
what is left of the summer.

We take inventory
of what's been gained and lost,
run mazes of promises made and kept.

The season's last nights
are counted like stars, like grains of sand,
like tiny blessings—

like how many more days the leaves
can hold on before
they fall.

Saved

Sometimes I think about
quitting my job / moving
to a mountain / shouting
poetry off its peak / summoning
the thin air to swallow me
like a snowstorm / to make me
feel something / to make me
believe I am somehow
saved.

Soliloquy

For the life of me
I can't decide:

is it a celebration or
a tragedy

that every time
you slip through
my hands

poetry
falls in my lap
and makes a home of me.

Then again,
I have always craved
the eye of the storm
more than
the calm of the sea.

Feet of Fall

I dreamt once
that I was laying at the feet
of fall — its gold and green arms
reaching out to me
like something that needed
saving.

I never said it aloud
to anyone, but,
it was the other way
around.

October First

October's first sky
cracks open.

I wander into the morning,
wonder

whether we can
coexist.

Me

Summer turns to autumn
and autumn turns to winter
and winter turns to spring
and spring turns to summer
and

I'm
    still
        me.

November Elfchen

November
Autumn rises
sheds my skin
poetry falls from me
rebirthed

Rollercoasters

I have always considered myself
an adventurer.

I don't scuba dive
or parasail
or skydive but
I wear my heart
on my sleeve,
my words as tattoos
on my skin—

and willingly ride the rollercoasters
that come with it.

Good Morning

The morning greets me.

The sky's eyes are glittering;
the wind whistles
at my back.

Everything here is good.

Elephant in the Room

Winter, dressed in white,
slow-crawls across
empty streets—
neither a stranger
nor welcome
here.

Final Lines

There's a quiet calm
in knowing
the final lines of my story
have not yet been
written.

About the Author

Nicholas Olah draws on his love of nature and photography as his main inspirations for writing. He enjoys walking around his home in the Chicago suburbs and watching the colors change during each of the four distinct Midwest seasons.

Nicholas has previously self-published two collections, Where Light Separates from Dark and Which Way is North.

Check out his work at www.nicholasolah.com.

Made in the USA
Monee, IL
15 March 2022